Poems for Fifty Years

Also by Graham Swift

The Sweet Shop Owner
Shuttlecock
Learning to Swim
Waterland
Out of This World
Ever After
Last Orders
The Light of Day
Tomorrow
Making an Elephant
Wish You Were Here
England and Other Stories
Mothering Sunday
Here We Are
Twelve Post-War Tales

Poems for Fifty Years

Graham Swift

SCRIBNER

London · New York · Amsterdam/Antwerp · Sydney/Melbourne · Toronto · New Delhi

First published in Great Britain by Scribner, an imprint of Simon & Schuster UK Ltd, 2026
All poems and preface © 2009 Graham Swift and published in *Making an Elephant*,
first published in Great Britain by Picador, an imprint of Pan Macmillan, 2009

1 3 5 7 9 10 8 6 4 2

Simon & Schuster UK Ltd, 7th Floor
199 Bishopsgate, London, EC2M 3TY

Simon & Schuster Australia, Sydney
Simon & Schuster India, New Delhi

www.simonandschuster.co.uk
www.simonandschuster.com.au
www.simonandschuster.co.in

A CIP catalogue record for this book is available from the British Library

Hardback ISBN: 978-1-3985-6742-9
eBook ISBN: 978-1-3985-5606-5
eAudio ISBN: 978-1-3985-5607-2

The authorised representative in the EEA is Simon & Schuster Netherlands BV,
Herculesplein 96, 3584 AA Utrecht, Netherlands. info@simonandschuster.nl

Typeset in Garamond by M Rules

Printed and Bound in the UK using 100% Renewable Electricity at CPI Group (UK) Ltd

Poems for Fifty Years

Introduction

The poems in this book first appeared, rather covertly, in *Making an Elephant*, my only book of non-fiction pieces and my only book aspiring to be a kind of autobiography. In the book's introduction I said that I wasn't sure if poetry counted as fiction or non-fiction, and that the poems weren't meant to be the filler in a sandwich constructed mainly of prose. These were valid remarks, though I regret likening any book to a sandwich. The poems were given their own separate preface, and the original preface follows here.

The poems were, at the time, my only excursion into poetry and they remain so now, seventeen years after *Making an Elephant* was published. A further peculiarity was that they were all written, in something of a spate, in 2004, after I'd finished one of my novels and was awaiting the germ of the next. That's to say, for a short, intense period of my life I wrote nothing but poetry. This had never occurred before and has never occurred since. The original preface offers its view on this, which I wouldn't want to alter. In the end, with any kind of creative writing, you can't account for how things—just happen.

That I can't account for how the poems arose doesn't mean that I think they were an aberration. Revisiting them now, I feel that they exhibit in a compressed way things that have concerned me constantly as a writer of fiction: the wish to penetrate our inner lives while at the same time registering the broad effects of history and social change—all combined with the abiding urge to tell a story.

In short, the poems seem to belong not just to a freakish period in 2004 but to my whole working life. At any rate, they are expressive of it. Though written in a short space of time, they are poems of a lifetime, and lifetimes are what some of them attempt to encapsulate. In 2004 I was nearing the end of my third decade as a published writer. I've now reached the end of my fifth. To mark this half century, it seemed fitting for my only foray into poetry to appear at last in unsandwiched form as a separate volume. One of the subjects of the poems is undoubtedly time, and time is, undoubtedly, one of the subjects of my fiction. Fifty years is quite a serious chunk of time, and I hope this book of poems will stand the test of time, along with all my other books.

GS 2026

Original Preface 2009

In the misty and often lengthy periods which I later come to realize are the preludes to my starting a new book, I've noticed that my reading can shift from novels, or anything large, to poetry, as if I'm aware that whatever I do next will arise not from any grand design but from some small, insistent vibration; a blink of light through the fog.

I'll often concentrate on the poems of just one poet and even be drawn (though there's not such a wide field) to poets better known for their prose. Raymond Carver's poems, for example, have sometimes been my companions in the mist, and it would be true to say that I've derived more from them than from his widely admired stories. The poems give me that feeling of being in the same space as the man, which in these obscure intervals seems to be what I need.

Just once, so far, has this temporary inclination for reading poetry toppled over into writing it. Some months after I completed *The Light of Day* I found myself, unexpectedly, writing little else. One poem seemed to lead to another, so that I acquired, until it suddenly stopped, the cautiously darting momentum (quite unlike the momentum of writing a novel) with which you hop from stepping stone to stepping stone. That suggests it all had some transitional purpose, though I think it was more a case of not wanting to feel, while I waited for a new novel to loom, creatively becalmed. Perhaps it was just refreshing to be making those quick, frequent leaps. Novels come with gaps between them too, and I wouldn't want to say that there's any particular purpose or pattern to the way they're interspersed, just as I can't really explain how I make the larger leaps—or rather, slow, tentative journeys—between them. In the end, after a gap, they just happen. These are some of the poems that, in one of the gaps, just happened too.

This Small Place

The world is big enough,
Though getting smaller, they say,
And as for the universe—let's not think of that.
But there's always this small place, close to hand,
This place of small talk and whispers and memories
And small mercies and small blessings,
And small comfort, true enough, sometimes.
We started here, and now and then
We've come back, only half meaning to,
But thankful enough to find it still there,
In the small hours,
With only some furniture and our thoughts.
And it's where we'll be at the finish,
We know this too,
Sure enough, true enough, big enough.

Waves

When we all gather together,
Get thrown together, at bashes and dos,
I think of the seaside, the gleeful light,
Of how we've all gone in for a dip and, beyond the
    sparkling froth,
There are big waves running and
Up and down we go,
Up and down.
Those moments when we laugh at each other to see it:
Up and down!
Those moments when a wave slaps us, mid-laugh,
And we gulp and panic a little but laugh again.
Those moments when between the crests and troughs
We lose sight of each other altogether.

Our Childhoods

They pluck us on the shoulder sometimes.
Remember us?
And we think of them
Perplexedly, if fondly,
As if we don't know who they really are.
And yet we know something they don't know:
That really they're orphans, all orphans.
Look at them there, up to their old tricks.
When will they find out?
And then, when they have, who will they become?

Rush Hour

The fog of their massed breath,
The still-sleepy glitter of their eyes.
So this is their life, what they do every day,
Funnelled into work like hour-glass sand?
No, no, look again. It's not what it seems.
This smoky-blue dawn
That hasn't yet torn them from dreams,
These lights on their faces.
Not regulars, but extras, taking their places,
Here for this one, unrepeatable scene.

To His Dead Father

Their age freezes, but we go on,
Burning the years.
If I could meet him now
There wouldn't be that gap between us.
I'd say, 'I'm catching up,'
Like someone adjusting
To the other's brisker pace.
I'd say, 'I see it now like you saw it.
The thing is, I just lagged behind.'
We'd walk, we'd talk, we'd know each other.
We'd be like equals, brothers, friends.

Inmates

School dormitories, barrack rooms,
Hospital wards and, by a stretch,
Prison wings too.
All of a muchness and all grim.
But imagine them empty,
All the narrow beds unburdened.
Thrown in, we learn the hard way to muck in too,
All fondly supposing there's some other free place
Where we're all tender autocrats,
All sweet, proud exceptions to the rules.
And so it should be.
But, still, imagine them empty:
The long spaces silent,
Not a door being swung,
The beds simply waiting, as if no one's said,
The cold sheets taut, undented,
All the meaningless lights-outs.

History

The child is father to the man, they say,
And sometimes you can have the fancy
That all the creatures of history are children.
We are the only sad, wise grown-ups now.
To have lived in their day!
On a sledge, say, in St Petersburg, in 1904.
Or on the old ranch, out west,
Before Pearl Harbor, chasing the kicking maverick,
Watching the still wet foal find its legs.
Those simple, carefree times!

Borrowers

Who'd have credited it fifty years ago?
This genie in our wallet:
Yes, o master, it shall be so.
Was it a trick perhaps, we thought at first,
But, 'Live now, pay later,' came the cry
And, not to be left out, we took it up
With interest. Look at us living now.
So does that mean for those who came before
The rule was: Pay now, live later?
So it seems. Poor fools.
Life was always over the rainbow then.
And some of them paid the highest price
And never lived later at all,
Lying where they do
In Africa, Burma, Italy or France
Or where all the dreamed-of treasure lies,
If not over the rainbow, under the sea.
Credit where it's due, but they never knew
The sweet scam of living on it.
Judy Garland made them cry,
Madonna made us buy.

And the ones still left from those sad days
Shuffle now round Happy Homes, or,
Worse, wait bedless in some corridor,
Their cheated faces saying, I paid, I paid—for this.
So how shall it be for us
When our day of reckoning comes?
Having had our run of plastic bliss
Shall we all topple nobly,
Smiling fair's-fair smiles,
Into the black pit? Singing as we go,
Oh but we lived, boy, how we lived,
Bye-bye.

The Virtuoso

Sometimes, now it's impossible,
Now it's all useless,
He pines not for the great days,
The tours, the concert halls,
The roar of orchestras and applause,
But for days, long ago,
When he'd make his way
To the Academy. Some crisp morning
In autumn that seemed there
Just for him. Leaves on the cobbles.
The sun glittering along alleyways.
People passing, muffled, gloved,
In little clouds of steam.
His own hands, of course, were mittened,
And held, before he left (his mother
Filled the bowl), in hot water.
He'd hug them, even so,
Under his armpits. On Wilhelmstrasse
The tram bells rang.
Mornings he'd feared and loved.
One of those mornings (it was all still a dream)

When he'd climb those stone stairs,
Enter that tall, stern, merciless chamber,
Take up his instrument,
Take up his bow,
And (why *this* morning, what
Was magic about *this* morning?)
Everything sang.

We Both Know

We both know, we both knew.
It hovers now around us when we meet
Like some trick of light.
And those images of what might have been
Can't be so different now
From images of things that really were,
Memory and longing amounting to the same.
Our eyes meet. We never say, we never will.
Is this the sweetest, surest thing, in fact?
A poise, a tact unknown to the young.
We burned but never were consumed,
This soft ash keeping in the fire.

Breadcrumbs

Once, just glancing through the window
(Why should it have fixed him in his place?)
He saw his wife, with breadcrumbs for the birds,
Standing at the kitchen door.
Just a woman in a doorway with a breadboard,
A streak of sunlight, on a dull day, touching her hair,
But also his wife.
She never looked up to catch his stare.
Now that she's gone from his life
And he doesn't know what to do with the years,
He walks round galleries, and before
Those pictures painted by the Dutch—
Bits of yards, bits of rooms, a door, a figure,
Bits of nothing much—
He finds it hard to choke the tears.

The Trespasser

He never could quite grasp it,
A boy in school assembly:
'Forgive us our trespasses . . .'
What kind of word was that?
He only understood the sense
That had to do with property,
Or with not being on it.
Trespassers were people
Who *weren't supposed to be there.*
And wasn't that, he knew by then,
Exactly where he was at?
An intruder in this place:
Common mishap of us all.
And wasn't that the simple trick of it,
To know that you'd be always
On the wrong side of the fence?
He knew it even as he mumbled
Through those morning prayers,
Meek expression on his face.
It led him to a life (as he would call
It later) of 'adventure':

Con man and wife-stealer to the gentry,
Maestro of the sham,
Always creeping over someone else's carpet,
Always stealing down someone else's stairs
(Always stealing anyway).
Not a 'stranger in this world', as some
Weird people liked to say,
Oh no, but just a trespasser.

Chekhov at Melikhovo

Of course, a doctor, he knew.
He'd never grow old.
All through those quick June nights
The yellow light burned in his window
While the moths danced in and out
And the scent of hay and honeysuckle
Failed to distract him.
As if he needed, for his true mania,
These mere remissions in the summer fever,
This cool, dark flavour of brevity.
And he'd sleep, anyway, like a dead weight,
Like some useless *thing*,
Through the long boring fire of day.

Watched

Once, there were our parents to watch over us
And God, of course (we were told), looking down,
And it was a comfort bigger than we knew then,
Not to know the loneliness which we know now
Of our own devices.
To be watched. Isn't that the trick?
Isn't that the knack of those characters
Up there on the screens,
To whom we glue our eyes?
They are watched—we ourselves confirm it.
They have us to turn to, us to thank.
If only *life* had an audience, a theatre for each one of us.
Watched. Saved.

Extinction

What do ten vanished species of moth or mollusc
Matter to you or me?
The world will have gone before it is gone.
Or the hieroglyphics of the ancients?
Or even the quaint anachronism of a still-current phrase?
'Changing horses in midstream.'
Leave all that to the specialists and saddos.
We're not special, you and I,
Or sad.
The world will have gone before it is gone.

The Anatomist

Of course he remembers it,
The funeral, the procession, the crowds
And (as if by command) a weeping sky.
In those days even the weather adopted style.
Of course he remembers. The great weight
Of importance, like those pressing clouds,
That somehow he had to shoulder now—
'Brave little man', as they called him.
Only six, but how could he forget?
His mother's hand clutching his (everyone
Noticed that), as if he had to steady *her*.
And later, in private, her hugs, her tears,
As if he were some leftover part of *him*.
But she married again inside two years.
And that, really, was the whole story:
The young wife, from the beginning,
There to adorn her husband's glory.
And that's why there'd been that gap not just
Of decades but of pretty well everything
Between himself and him. Six years!
'But aren't you proud?' they'd say. 'You must

Be proud to have been his son.' And yes,
He'd say, for decency's and simplicity's sake.
Though pride never really came into it,
Except, maybe, on that grey, wet morning,
The plumed horses stamping and steaming
(How like a fairy tale it would one day seem).
But mostly what he felt was the great, grey yawning
Of his own decades stretched before him.
How could they be anything but lesser, small?
Not pride, not pride at all.

And when, later, they came, the biographers
And researchers, asking for his memories,
His 'child's-eye view', he had the perfect
Excuse. It was never exactly like lying.
I was only six, he'd stress, and he was always—though
Don't get me wrong—a rather distant figure.
He didn't say: What I remember is a man dying.
That house, that dreadful room, that bed.
It was a long slow illness, you know,
Not a 'valiant battle' like the papers said.
What I actually remember is a wasting, shrinking
Body, what happens (but I was only small)
To any mortal human animal.

Later, as it turned out (raised by a grudging
Aunt, who had her secret viewpoint too),
He took up medicine. Or not medicine so much
As that strictly scientific stuff: anatomy, pathology.
Became not undistinguished in his way.
Students would whisper now and then

(There was nothing he could do about the name):
Yes, he's the son. But he would always say,
Offering them his prefatory remark or two:
What, ladies and gentlemen, is our study?
It's the study, ladies and gentlemen,
Of how we're all the same.

Civilization

Would you have it any other way?
This cosy collusion in the trivial,
Much fuss and much indecision,
Then much preening
Over a new pair of shoes.
You want drum rolls and proclamations
And noble leanings?
Would you have it any other way?

Unlooked-for

These moments that come like gifts,
Ordinary moments that aren't so ordinary at all.
Like the sun on a cool day
Suddenly warming your neck.
My God, this is all you could wish,
Simple unlooked-for heaven.
While a thousand engineered occasions,
A thousand worked-at culminations fail.
Once, perhaps, you'd hardly have noticed.
You'd have rolled your shoulders, pettishly,
Under this unsolicited kiss.
Just life, for God's sake,
It's just what life brings,
Plenty more of this.
Now you're not so foolish.
You do the second, the double-blessed thing,
You heed it, mark it,
This unremarkable bliss.

Affection

And affection too.
Not love, it's true, no fires within,
Just simple affection, flickering from skin to skin.
Not lust or seduction or desire or possession,
Just simple affection,
Warming the air in between.

There Without Us

We've all been to such places,
Where the brambles shudder in the wind
And the branches creak up above
And rain batters the leaves.
We went there once when that sudden squall
Held up our summer walk,
And waited, watching everything
As you eye the furniture in a stranger's room,
And thought: we're here now and might never have been
And soon won't be, and places such as these,
Pierced with birds and secret life,
Must hardly ever get or need a human visitor.
It must be there still, while this rain beats
On the window. We think of it suddenly:
That place where we stood once
Under sighing trees—
The smell of roots and deep earth,
As if our nostrils were required for it—
And think of all such places
That are there without us now,
All the places where we've been but haven't.

Homings

Salmon still passage through the estuaries,
Geese arrow the heavens,
Turtles tunnel the oceans.
When shall we tell them we have ravaged their mysteries?
Whom shall we choose as our spokesman?

Priam

Maybe we all end up like Priam,
Not one of the heroes wreathed in glory,
Just the man who gets to be king of Troy,
Father of a hot-headed, cock-happy boy
Who steals a wife and starts a war.
The usual wretched soap-opera story.
But at your level it has to mean more,
So just when you've made your pile and settled down
And built your topless towers of Ilium,
You've a siege on your hands and now, what's more,
This crazy *horse* outside your front door.
Was it for this you strove and pushed your luck,
Just to get pulled back into the muck?
Who, given the choice, would be a king?
But you were, and you took it.
Now here's this weirdest thing:
A lull, a silence everywhere. A horse.
You look around, you stroke your royal chin. Of course.
Maybe you had your glory all the time,
And this is what it means: you win.
A horse. It's not your common sort of offering.
Maybe it stands for you, for Priam in his kingly prime.
Best take a look, best take it in.

The Bookmark

All the books you meant to read
Or reread or try again,
Having tried once long ago and failed:
There they sit, spurned, on your shelves.
And one wet weekend you actually reach
For an old crinkly-spined paperback and settle down,
But something stops you before you've begun:
The bus ticket falling from page thirty-one.
A bus ticket, yellowed and frail,
Like the pages themselves.
And what do you do?
You read the bus ticket, not the book,
Marvelling at its weird historicality,
The story it seems to want to tell.
Bus tickets don't come like that any more,
Nor at that price. You wonder what
The journey was for such a fictional fare.
From where to where? And when?
But mostly you puzzle who the person was
Who bought this ticket and instead of doing
All the annihilating things that are done

To bus tickets, slipped it casually
Yet fatefully, like a message in a bottle,
Between the pages of a never reopened novel.
You're lost in the bus ticket, you forget the book.
You know, of course, it must have been you.

Touch

Where do we really live?
Where is the centre of command?
In our eyes? Our brains?
In this thing that beats in our chest?
Or is it in our hands?
Those canny little twins,
So good at fending for themselves,
We can almost forget they're there.
Nothing speaks more
Of our time here than our hands.
Look how they weather and gnarl.
A hand is like a face (and sometimes lovelier)
And what can a face *do*, make, mend?
A hand has a mind, a memory surer
Than that stuff in our heads:
Ask any musician or draughtsman.
And what, in a word, do all wise masters teach
Their daunted apprentices?
Your hands will do it, give it time,
Your hands will tell you what to do.
Aren't we all apprentices to our hands?

And isn't the true mastery in touch?
Think of it, now you've come this far.
Look at your faithful hands.
Aren't *you* the faithful one, led like the blind
By those things before your eyes?
Think of all the moments, all the tests.
How many times, over and over,
Have those dumb creatures
Instructed you in the art of life?
How to reach out and do exactly what is needed.
How to comfort, caress, cherish, punish, beg.

The Dead

They cry to us, never finding the words
To tell us what we already know,
That our own lost voices will one day
Be as theirs, the mouths of our souls
Gaping like graves, gaping for reunion
With those we have preceded.

On the Bridge

Three girls on a bridge
(A subject for a painting—Gauguin or Munch).
Three girls on the old, quiet, stone bridge
At the edge of the little town
Where he, an English academic driving south
(Some summer thing in Nîmes),
Decided to put up for the night
And after a meal and a *pichet* of *rouge*
To take a stroll in the late, soft light.
Swallows skimmed the little river,
Then on the bridge (the obvious place,
After crossing, to turn back),
Those three girls in a huddle at the centre,
Leaning on the parapet.
That moment of polite hiatus when
Two worlds meet and agree upon
The brief suspension of each.
A bridge. *'Bonsoir.' 'Bonsoir monsieur!'*

He felt an intruder, of course.
Should he have crossed at all?

Their bridge, not his. But then
He was hardly Actaeon
Crashing on the forest pool.
And which, in any case, was Diana,
Which the attendant nymphs?
The fact is they were, all three, beauties—
And perhaps, somehow, he should have *said*.
Not intrusion but privilege.
Not Actaeon but Paris, come to judge.
(What was in that *pichet* of red?)

'Bonsoir monsieur!'
He crossed, walked on,
Turning along the farther bank,
Daring only once to twist his head
And see their faces still perched there,
Looking back at him, neither playful nor stern,
Just something in between.

Schoolgirls-no-more, he guessed:
The summer after the very last term,
And now they hung somewhere
Between girlhood and what comes next,
Looking for their futures perhaps
In the slow slide of the river.

The soft splash of a fish.
Their soft, indecipherable voices
Reached him over the water, and yes
(Somehow he knew it for them):
All their lives, they'd never forget.

These in-between places
Where all seems yet to come,
Which yet turn out to be the thing itself.
Do you remember, when we met?
Those evenings, that summer,
On the bridge.

Allotments

I used to tease out the word
Before I knew what it meant.
How could it be a lot when it looked so little?
A strip of soil for beans or cabbages,
A cold frame, a compost heap.
Hardly the Earth.
But look at the love that has gone into each.
The careful rows of canes,
The sheds magicked up from old offcuts,
Each one architecturally unique.
Look at them here on Sunday afternoons
Lost in their little worlds.
I never knew what a lot meant, or a little.
Then I was let in on the meaning.
'Allotment': it's what you get,
It's what you're given to get on with.
Didn't you understand?
Your little patch, your little place,
Among all the others.

Perspective

The desire to be in and out of your skin,
That soft fatal voice, yours and not yours,
That says even as you walk down the street:
'He walked down the street.'
This damp paving, these walls,
These rooftops, drying against a brightening sky,
Aren't of now, and only ever will be
Of some time that was.
Understand your position.
Understand the anguish of the painter
Who long ago in some Flemish town
Looked from his window and painted what he saw
So it would remain, in its frame,
Like another window on another world.

Relapse

These things that were still *there*,
Like scorched flowers under winterloads of ice,
These things that, surely, you could never relive.
But most of his life had fallen away
Like meaningless waste,
Memory caving in, an avalanche of the brain,
And he was back there again
Among that mountainous furniture,
Among those towering creatures,
Like some small, pecking bird
Hopping among buffalo, elephants.
Adults! What great, alien beasts they were.
And he'd been one once!
Their huge, crashing weight
And their thick, leathery stink of time.

Another

To see ourselves as others see us:
That's one thing.
But to see others when they don't see us,
When they aren't just part of our own grey penumbra,
In their own sweet, bright, unshadowed space:
That's another.

This Is the Life

'This is the life, eh?' some cheery oaf said,
In cravat and blazer and seaside flannels.
And of course we thought he was a fool.
But is *this* the life then, this life we've settled for?
No (we half know it), this isn't the life either.
And there he stands, that oaf, on the jetty,
Getting smaller.
He hasn't realized yet: we're *leaving*, not arriving.
There he stands, still grinning and waving
And rubbing his hands in readiness,
Trousers flapping in the wind.